DANGEROUS CATCH!

DEEP SEA FISHERS

Katelyn Rice

Consultants

Timothy Rasinski, Ph.D.
Kent State University

Lori Oczkus
Literacy Consultant

John Lee Levins Jr.
Fisherman

Based on writing from
TIME For Kids. TIME For Kids and the *TIME For Kids* logo are registered trademarks of TIME Inc. Used under license.

Publishing Credits

Dona Herweck Rice, *Editor-in-Chief*
Lee Aucoin, *Creative Director*
Jamey Acosta, *Senior Editor*
Heidi Fiedler, *Editor*
Lexa Hoang, *Designer*
Stephanie Reid, *Photo Editor*
Sandy Phan, *Contributing Author*
Rachelle Cracchiolo, *M.S.Ed., Publisher*

Image Credits: Cover, pp.1, 28–29, 37 (bottom right), 45 Getty Images; p.47 (bottom) Klas Stolpe/Associated Press; p.36 The Marine Stewardship Council; p.41 William B. Folsom, NMFS/NOAA; pp.22, 23 Lee Aucoin; p.47 (top) U.S. Navy; pp.42–43, 48–49, 49 U.S. Coast Guard; pp.8–9, 12–13, 18, 20–21, 30–31, 52–53 (illustrations) J.J. Rudisill; All other images from Shutterstock.

Teacher Created Materials

5301 Oceanus Drive
Huntington Beach, CA 92649-1030
http://www.tcmpub.com
ISBN 978-1-4333-4943-0
© 2013 Teacher Created Materials, Inc.

TABLE OF CONTENTS

ROUGH SEAS

*Thirty-foot waves and 60-**knot** winds toss the ship in the air. The crew bashes ice off the side of the boat and pushes fishing gear overboard. They must reduce their weight or risk rolling over and sinking!*

Deep sea fishers spend weeks and sometimes months at sea. They may face severe weather and other dangers with only their fellow crew members to rely on. Damaged equipment, injury, and death are very real risks in this **profession**. But deep sea fishers would take a stormy sea over an office job any day. They seek adventure and challenge. They work as a team, putting their lives on the line, always waiting for the next big catch.

THINK LINK

→ What techniques do deep sea fishers use to make a catch?

→ What types of boats and equipment do fishers use?

→ How do fishers deal with dangers on the job?

Fishing Forefathers

Fishing is one of the oldest professions in the world. For thousands of years, people have looked to the sea for food. Ancient cultures around the world left behind discarded shells, bones, and fishing hooks. Cave paintings show that fishing has been important to people for thousands of years.

Most early fishing was done with traps and nets in shallow water. Some ancient fishers caught fish with clubs and spears. American Indians also caught fish with lines and hooks made out of animal bones. Small boats were used in deeper waters. As boats and equipment improved, people moved into deeper ocean areas.

Waves of Fishing

Early fishing was done in lakes. As new techniques were developed, fishers were able to move into larger, more dangerous bodies of water. The bravest fishers tested the waters first. When they returned home alive, others were happy to follow them on their next trip out to sea.

Modern Fishing

Ancient Fishing

Prehistoric Fishers

In 2011, thousands of fish bones were found in a cave on the island of East Timor. Scientists say the fish were caught 42,000 years ago. They believe ancient Southeast Asian islanders may have used nets and hooks on long lines thrown into deep waters.

7

Tricks of the Trade

Fishing in wild waters takes skill and preparation. Deep sea fishers are the hunters of the sea. They use a variety of techniques to make a catch. Some use special boats or try to attract fish with **bait**. Others fish in remote areas. Some boats are designed to find fish and scoop them up as they swim by. Often fish are **lured** to the site with small bits of food. It's a difficult life, and fishers need every advantage they can get.

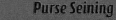

Purse Seining

is named after a drawstring purse. A net from a larger boat is drawn by a smaller boat around a school of fish.

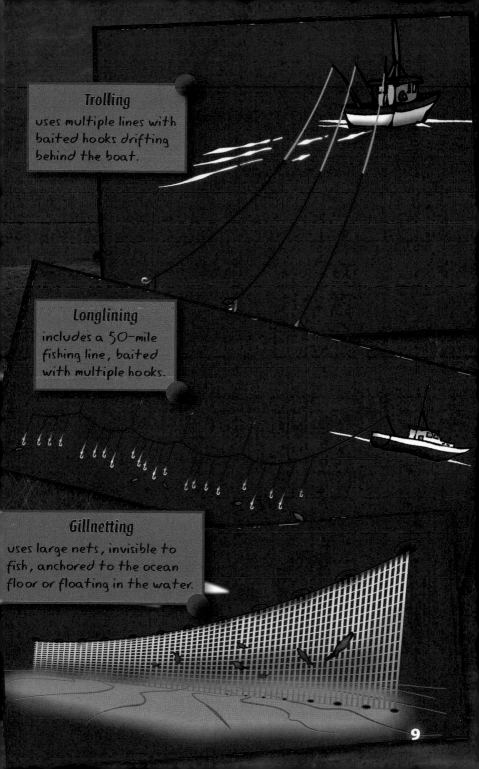

Trolling
uses multiple lines with baited hooks drifting behind the boat.

Longlining
includes a 50-mile fishing line, baited with multiple hooks.

Gillnetting
uses large nets, invisible to fish, anchored to the ocean floor or floating in the water.

Working on the Water

There's no time to rest on a **commercial** deep-sea **vessel**. Fishers set out and haul in nets and traps. They sort the catch, throwing back unwanted fish and marine animals. They also clean the boat and take turns cooking meals. Whether it's sharpening the hooks or preparing the bait, there's always something to do. Most importantly, everything must be done carefully and quickly. A crew member who gets tangled up in ropes on the deck and falls overboard could be lost forever.

"Everything from the biggest detail to the smallest detail can and will kill you."
—Steven Snider, commercial fisher

The Law of the Sea

International laws are designed to cover the oceans of the world. The law of the sea notes which country controls each body of water. Fishing boats are not allowed to operate within about 200 **nautical miles** of a foreign country. (A nautical mile is 1.15 miles on land)

Learning the Lingo

To become a deep sea fisher, you need to learn the ropes—and the lingo. Being able to tell the difference between the bow and the stern could save your life!

bow—the front of the boat

port—the left side of the boat

starboard— the right side of the boat

stern—the back of the boat

batten down—to tie or secure all loose objects on the boat

ballast—weight placed at the bottom of the boat to keep it stable

chummer—someone who is seasick

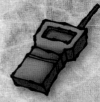

emergency position indicating radio beacon (EPIRB)—a device that sends out a signal for rescuers to use to find your location

global positioning system (GPS)—a radio receiver that uses satellite signals to find a location

in the meat pile—in an area with a large amount of fish or crab

sound navigation ranging (SONAR)—a way to detect objects underwater, using sound waves

Boat Basics

On the water, a boat is a factory, a house, and an office all in one. The best boats make fishing as **efficient** as possible. Ships need to be able to catch large quantities of fish to make the work worthwhile. The best ships can be operated with a small crew. The weight and size of the engine must be considered. Fuel costs should be low, and a good ship can go fast when necessary. The captain must consider where the boat will be used. Narrow **straits** and icy waters may require boats that have special features. The captain must also check that a vessel can handle difficult weather. Above all, safety is a top priority.

Hitchhikers

Like gum on the bottom of a shoe, marine growth on the bottom of a boat can slow it down! For better fuel efficiency, boats need to occasionally be freed of barnacles and weeds.

Ship-Shape Materials

Boats can be built from a variety of materials.

Steel is the most common material. It is usually used on larger vessels.

Wood is more expensive and used less than in the past.

Fiberglass is being used in smaller boats.

Aluminum is lightweight and long lasting.

Specialized Boats

On the water, life is all about the catch. That's why special boats are built to catch different types of fish. Trawlers have powerful engines. Large nets hang from the decks and are dragged through the water. Seiners have massive cranes to lift heavy nets filled with fish. Lift-netter boats catch fish by lowering nets over the side and luring the fish into the nets with bright lights. These boats are best for short trips because they are less powerful. Longliners are large boats with hooks and fishing lines trailing behind the boat. Fishers bait the hooks and pull the fish onto the boat. Many boats are designed to handle multiple types of equipment. This way, they can be used to catch a variety of fish.

Factory trawlers are the largest fishing vessels. They can be over 300 feet long and hold over 50 crew members!

What's in a Name?

Some believe that ancient Egyptians started the tradition of naming boats. It is a tradition continued around the world today. For many boat owners, it takes years to come up with the right name. Gods and goddesses, planets, celebrities, and many other things inspire boat names. People also choose silly names for their boats. *Knot Lost*, *Marlin Monroe*, *Vitamin Sea*, and *Prawn To* are just a few!

Egyptian ships date back 5,000 years to 3,000 BC

On Deck

Commercial boats are built to handle large quantities of fish. These are tough ships that can withstand harsh waters for weeks on end. Every area of the boat helps fishers do their job or keeps them safe.

After catching and sorting, fish are moved to the processing deck.

Large crews of workers can live on the boat.

Large nets are stored on reels.

Frozen fish is stored in the hold.

Mother Ships

Some factory trawlers act as the lead ship in a group of smaller boats. They store and process the fish that is caught by other boats. This allows the smaller vessels to focus on hauling in more catches without going back to port.

High-Tech Fishing

Fishing has come a long way from wooden spears and small traps in a lake. Modern equipment helps crews make the most of their time on the water. And a simple error message on a computer screen can mean the difference between success and failure.

Most of the action may happen on the deck of a boat, but the **wheelhouse** is where the ship's captain works. The wheelhouse includes **navigation** and **communication** tools. The **autopilot** controls the steering. The GPS feeds information to the autopilot. It keeps the ship on course. Computers help the crew spot any problems with the fishing gear. Sensors note the position of the nets and lines. SONAR is used to detect fish. Radio and satellite equipment also help locate fish.

Sound pulses, or radio waves, are beamed down from the ship.

Radio waves reflect, or echo back, to the ship from a school of fish.

SONAR results show the size, quantity, and movement of the fish.

inside the wheelhouse

Gearing Up

In a winter storm, the right gear can mean the difference between a successful catch and a miserable day on the water. It's all about staying dry. The professionals cover their bodies from head to toe, but they still never seem to stay completely dry. Some crew members store gear in every port. That way, wherever they are in the world, they will be ready to suit up and hit the water!

A heavy parka protects the body. A hood is useful in windy or rainy conditions.

Reflective tape makes it easier to spot a fisher who has fallen overboard.

Gloves protect hands from the cold and heavy lifting. Inside, cotton liners add another layer of warmth.

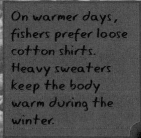

On warmer days, fishers prefer loose cotton shirts. Heavy sweaters keep the body warm during the winter.

Slickers are worn during food processing.

Wide legs make it easy to take pants on and off over boots.

The fabric is coated to resist water and oil. It stays flexible even in extremely cold temperatures.

Most fishers keep an extra pair of boots on hand. If one pair gets wet, there's a dry pair ready for the next day.

23

In the Danger Zone

While boats are looking for fish, some creatures are looking for boats. Dolphins and whales are often drawn to the sound of boats. They swim alongside the ships. This friendly behavior can turn dangerous for them if they get caught in the nets.

REEL IT IN

The ocean is **vast**. There are hundreds, if not thousands, of good fishing sites around the world. But which spots are truly the best? Where are the biggest and tastiest fish? Asking the crew might not be much help. Just as magicians never reveal their secrets, the best fishers never reveal the best fishing spots.

Location, time, bait, and water depth are all examined when planning a fishing trip. Helicopters and airplanes may be used to spot large schools of fish. Porpoises often lead fishing boats to tuna. Birds diving into the water may also be a sign of fish nearby. Experts know that changes in the water's temperature, color, and current may indicate fish are in the water. Only when the conditions are right will a fishing trip **yield** a rewarding catch.

All Tapped Out

Even reliable fishing places can run out of fish quickly. Sometimes, this happens because too many fish have been caught. Other times, natural changes in the ocean currents or weather bring about change.

Location, Location, Location

The most expensive equipment in the world won't be any help if fishers don't know where to use it. Here are some popular hot spots fishers go when they need a big catch.

NORTH AMERICA

ATLANTIC OCEAN

PACIFIC OCEAN

SOUTH AMERICA

ARCTIC
OCEAN

EUROPE

ASIA

AFRICA

INDIAN
OCEAN

AUSTRALIA

SOUTHERN
OCEAN

ANTARCTICA

27

The Payoff!

The moment the traps and lines are pulled in is one of suspense. Will there be hundreds of fish or nothing at all? Fishers dump the traps or remove hooks and lures from the fish. Then, the catch is sent on a conveyor belt into a tank of water under the deck. Some boats store the haul on ice. Sometimes, the fish are gutted and sorted, but this is usually done at a **processing plant**.

What's the payoff for all this work? There can be a hundred large crabs in a trap. That's about 1,000 pounds of crab. And fishers can hope to earn about $5,000 from a single trap. With multiple traps, a crew might haul in $50,000 in a day, but that's only if luck is on their side.

Fishers work carefully and quickly to remove fish from a net pulled on board.

Lead the Way

While the crew works to haul in the fish, it's the captain's job to manage the boat. The captain is in charge of moving the boat safely as the crew slips and slides across the wet deck. It's important to control the boat so the traps and fishing lines aren't damaged. If the weather is rough, the captain aims the boat into calm waters to make it easier for the crew to work.

DIG DEEPER!

All Hands on Deck

A deep sea fishing boat's crew is a strong and brave team. Each member has a different role, but everyone pitches in on deck when needed. Cooking skills are a plus for every crewmember, as kitchen duty is often shared.

Captain

Also known as the *skipper*, the captain controls the boat. The captain decides where and when to fish. He or she has the most responsibility.

Deckhand

Most fishing boats have at least two deckhands. A deckhand guides the nets, traps, and lines. Deckhands haul and sort the catch. Some deckhands assist the engineer and later earn the rank of engineer.

First Mate

The first mate, or second captain, helps the captain control the boat. He or she takes over if something happens to the captain. The first mate manages and trains the deckhands.

Engineer

The engineer keeps the boat running smoothly. He or she takes care of the equipment in the engine room and on deck. The engineer also handles emergency repairs.

Greenhorn

The greenhorn is the least experienced member on board. He or she must be ready to pick up the slack and help out wherever needed. The greenhorn cleans the boat and baits the lines.

Fish Profiles

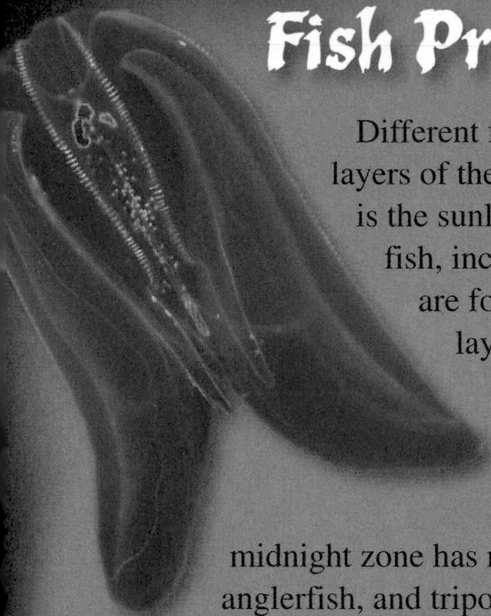

Different fish are found at different layers of the ocean. The top layer is the sunlight zone. Most ocean fish, including sharks and rays, are found there. The next layer is the twilight zone. Some whales, squid, jellyfish, crabs, and octopuses live in this cold, dark area. The midnight zone has no sunlight. The viperfish, anglerfish, and tripod fish in this layer have no eyes. **Bioluminescent** creatures are found in the darkest zones. The deep sea contains many amazing sea creatures humans have yet to discover!

SHARKS

RAYS

ANGLERFISH

A Heavy Load

Commercial fishing may also include capturing these non-fish:

- lobsters
- crabs
- prawns
- oysters
- sponge
- sea turtles

WHALES

SQUIDS

TRIPOD FISH

Overfishing

A great catch can change a fisher's life. But it can also change the ocean. Some marine species are disappearing because of **overfishing**. Overfishing happens when the stock, or numbers of a species, gets too low. This may happen because humans are fishing more than the ocean can produce. Fishing equipment and techniques also change marine **ecosystems**.

Large quantities of targeted fish are **harvested** and killed.

Overfishing changes the ecosystem, and fishing gear can ruin habitats.

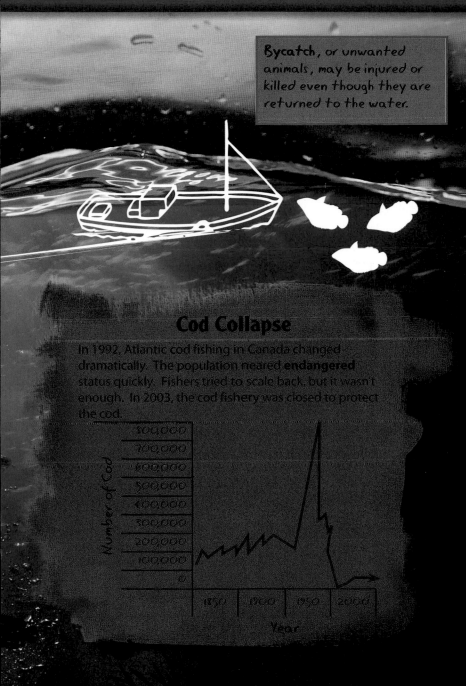

Bycatch, or unwanted animals, may be injured or killed even though they are returned to the water.

Cod Collapse

In 1992, Atlantic cod fishing in Canada changed dramatically. The population neared **endangered** status quickly. Fishers tried to scale back, but it wasn't enough. In 2003, the cod fishery was closed to protect the cod.

Sustainable Seafood

Some groups are working to stop overfishing. They want to support **sustainable** seafood. These groups work to rebuild fish stock. They also suggest new ways to harvest fish. Using these methods protects the sea, results in less bycatch, and kills more mature fish.

Marine watchdog groups also monitor **aquaculture** companies that farm fish. These groups enforce practices that are safe for the fish, humans, and the environment. Their research helps people know how to buy safe and sustainable seafood. They make everyone responsible for sustainability—from fishers to everyday consumers.

CERTIFIED SUSTAINABLE SEAFOOD
MSC
www.msc.org

Certified Seafood

Organizations like the Marine Stewardship Council certify seafood is environmentally friendly and sustainable. There are also labels that show a product is safe for sea animals.

Cycle of Sustainability

Governments set fishing guidelines and limits on catches to keep fish stock at safe levels and prevent harm to marine environments.

Government scientists collect data about fish stock.

Young fish have time to grow, and fish stock increases.

Data analysts suggest catch limits.

Agency members meet to set catch limits and guidelines.

Government agents watch to ensure fishers follow guidelines when they harvest.

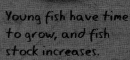

Floating Garbage

Fishing is only one of the factors affecting sea life. Weather is always a factor. On March 11, 2011, a **tsunami** swept across the eastern coast of Japan. Pieces of cars, trees, and houses were washed out to sea. When the floodwater **receded**, it pulled the **debris** into the Pacific Ocean. Scientists created the maps below to predict where the ocean currents would carry the debris over time.

The darkest areas on the maps represent areas with the most debris.

March 21, 2011

Japan   Portland
              Los Angeles

           Hawaii

March 2012

Japan   Portland
                          Los Angeles

              Hawaii

STOP! THINK...

- How long do experts predict it will take the debris to travel from Japan to the United States?

- Where are the densest areas of debris in each image?

- What American cities will receive the most debris?

Bird Bycatch

Fish aren't the only animals that get caught in fishers' traps. Sea birds dive for bait attached to long fishing lines. The birds are pulled underwater and drown. Some fishers avoid using weights on the nets to let birds or porpoises breathe on the surface of the water. The animals can survive until someone comes to set them free.

Young sharks have also been caught as bycatch.

Saving Sea Life

Fishers have begun using gear that reduces bycatch. Pingers emit sounds that keep dolphins and porpoises away. Reflective nets also **deter** porpoises. Fishers use special nets to allow unwanted species to leave the nets. Narrow holes trap smaller fish, and wider openings let out larger mammals. Fishers can also target fish by setting nets to close at certain times. The timing follows the daily patterns of the animal's movements. The companies that make fishing gear keep inventing new devices. Many seek to make fishing more efficient and safer for the planet.

This Bycatch Reduction Device (BRD) allows turtles to escape while shrimp are swept up.

What a Waste!

Fishers go out looking for a specific type of fish they know they can sell. But what comes back in the nets can be a mixed bag. Some fishing companies throw away more fish than they keep.

RISKS AND REWARDS

Deep sea fishers face many dangers. For a boat on the high seas, bad weather or equipment failure can spell disaster. The crew must be ready to handle anything—even a pirate attack! But the rewards may be worth the risks. If they make a good catch, the payoff can be very big.

Total Meltdown

There are many things that can go wrong on a boat. The engine can overheat. Computer monitors and electrical gear can malfunction. If the SONAR is down or water floods the equipment, it may be hard to control the vessel. Navigation and communication gear may break down. This could leave a ship lost with no way to call for help. Crew members should have a compass and portable radios. They should also know how to navigate by the stars. Boats are built to withstand heavy winds and harsh waves, but water has a way of damaging computers and other gear.

Mayday, Mayday!

If there is an emergency at sea, you can make a **distress call**. Special calls let others know exactly what kind of danger you're in.

Securité, securité, securité!

You are towing someone and want other boats to avoid you or let you know of any problems ahead.

Pan pan, pan pan, pan pan!

You have **run aground** and are slowly taking on water. Other boats may crash into you.

Mayday, mayday!

Your ship is sinking, you have lost a crew member overboard, your vessel is being attacked by pirates, or another serious emergency is occurring.

The United States Coast Guard is a military force that specializes in ocean rescue. It answers distress calls and enforces laws on the high seas.

22
21
20
19
18
17
16
15

Plimsoll line

In 1875, British parliament member Samuel Plimsoll created a law that continues to save lives on the sea. The law stated that a line must be painted on the sides of all ships. If the surface of the water rises above this line, then the ship's load is too heavy and the ship is in danger of sinking. This line became known as the *Plimsoll line*.

Survival packs on a fishing vessel include first-aid kits, radios, lights, beacons, flare guns, and flares. These should be stored in easy-to-reach places in case of an emergency.

Wild Weather

A seasoned fisher may know more about current weather conditions than a weather reporter. That's because fishers must study tides, water temperature, and winds to find the best catch. Their lives may depend on the weather. Fishing vessels often battle violent thunderstorms with heavy winds and rain. Waves can beat a boat against rocks. In the Bering Sea, frozen spray may coat a ship with ice. This can add extra weight to an already full deck of fishing equipment. A heavy boat can easily **capsize** on rough seas.

Suit Up!

If the ship goes down, a survival suit can protect fishers. When the suit is on, everything is covered except for the fisher's eyes. Its heavy material can keep someone from freezing to death in the water. And the bright color makes it easy for rescue teams to spot. New crew members are timed as they practice putting on the suit. If a ship is sinking, every second counts.

Modern Pirates

Pirates aren't a thing of the past. Unfortunately, they still **terrorize** the water. Modern pirates mainly attack cargo ships, but they also target fishing vessels. They **hijack** boats to resell or use in future attacks. Sometimes, pirates board a ship to demand cash or to kidnap crew members for **ransom**. Many pirates come from Somalia and Indonesia. Ships in pirate areas are often escorted by naval vessels for protection.

Getting Competitive

Pirate activity is illegal, but even legal boats can threaten success on the water. Fishing seasons for most seafood species only last a few months. With a short window of time to earn money for the entire year, fishers must work extra hard! Fishing vessels try to avoid one another, but competition can be fierce. Recently, stricter laws have limited catches. Once a boat has met a **quota** for the year, it must stop fishing for that species. This means boats are fighting over fewer fish.

Tricked at Sea

Pirates have many strategies for taking control of ships. They may set up distress flares to lure victims to them. Or one boat may attack from the front while other boats sneak up from behind. Armed pirates may even board a vessel as it slows down to enter a narrow waterway.

A Chance for Underdogs?

A law recently passed in Alaska may help smaller boats. The law limits the use of crab pots, reducing the number of crabs that can be caught at one time. Under this law, large ships that usually have the advantage will catch less at the beginning of a season. This may leave more crabs for smaller boats. This law also slows down and extends the crab season.

Sea Safety

Deep sea fishing is one of the most dangerous jobs in the world. Fishers can't afford to make mistakes, but experts estimate 80 percent of fishing accidents are caused by human error. Fishers feel pressure to score a big catch. They also worry about the competition. It can be easy to forget about safety.

Some fishers have begun taking safety courses. These programs teach fishers how to fight fires, control flooding, and survive in cold water. Fishers also learn how to safely abandon ship and save someone that falls overboard. To survive, a crew must always be prepared for the unexpected.

Risky Business

Fisher Steven Snider sailed on *The Captain Greg* during his first fishing trip. He stood on the deck as a shark was pulled in with the rest of the catch. As Snider stepped closer, the shark's jaws snapped closed around his left leg and clamped down. Despite the efforts of the crew, the shark would not release his leg. At least, not until they got out a **crowbar** to pry its jaw open!

United States Coast Guard trainees learn the correct way to enter a life raft from the water.

Top-Notch Training

Studies show the longer a fisher has been on the job, the more likely he or she is to have an accident. Experienced fishers often perform the more dangerous tasks on deck, and they may be more likely to take risks. Younger crew members are more likely to be trained in the latest safety procedures than older crew members.

At sea, something as simple as a hook in a hand can cause an infection. When a ship is far from land, it may be awhile before medical help arrives.

Big Bucks?

A commercial deep sea fisher can make anywhere from $5,000 to $100,000 each year. A very successful crab boat may rake in close to one million dollars in a season, but this is extremely rare. After the captain's share is taken out, the remaining profit from a catch, minus expenses, is split up among the rest of the crew.

Earning Votes

The first time a greenhorn fishes, the crew may vote on what they think he or she has earned. If the work was performed well, newbies may be invited back. The crew continues to vote on how much to pay less-experienced crew. Once a full share is granted, a fisher is considered a true peer.

$$\frac{\text{Total Earned - Captain's Share - Expenses}}{\text{Number of Crew Members}} = \text{Each Crew Member's Profit}$$

Captain: 45%
The captain usually owns the boat and receives the largest share of the profit.

Crew Member A: 10%
Each crew member earns a full share.

Crew Member B: 10%
30–36 percent of the total profit goes to crew members.

Total Earned

Crew Member C: 10%
Crew members include engineers and deckhands.

Greenhorn: 5%
The greenhorn earns a half-share.

Expenses: 20%
Expenses are taken out of the total earned. Expenses include the cost of fuel, oil, groceries, and gear.

Fish Market

A quick scan of the seafood section in a grocery store shows a variety of neatly skinned and sliced fish displayed on ice. Most consumers don't know what it takes to get these products to market. Fish are often more expensive than beef or chicken because fishing is such risky business. The risks fishers take are included in the cost of the fish. Fishers unload their catch at a processing plant either on land or at sea. Then, the sorted and gutted fish go to **distributors**. Next, local restaurants and stores stock their kitchens and seafood cases. Each step adds to the final price of the fish.

boat

processor

Baiting Online Buyers

Some fishers use the Internet to tell buyers about their fish. They can post photos and videos to raise interest in the latest catch.

On the Black Market

Many endangered marine species are caught and sold on the **black market**, despite catch limits. Some fishers underreport their harvests and illegally catch undersized fish. Atlantic salmon, striped bass, and bluefin tuna—a favorite of sushi lovers—are just a few of the species sold on the black market.

restaurant

grocery store

distributor

Surviving the Season

The stakes are high in commercial deep sea fishing. A successful season of work means food on the table at home and money in the bank. An unsuccessful season could mean injury or even death. Despite the dangers, fishers continue to make their living at sea. Every day on the water is a new adventure. Fishers brave the elements, stiff competition, and strict fishing laws. When they are at sea, they look forward to returning to their families. And some days, they just hope to live to see the next season.

Fisherman John Lee Levins Jr. hit land long enough to talk with writer Katelyn Rice about what makes deep sea fishing so amazing.

Katelyn: How did you become a deep sea fisherman?

John: My uncle Lee fished catfish in Lake Okeechobee in Florida when I was little. I loved to go out with him. Fishing became an addiction for me—like craving candy. Even later, when we moved to North Carolina, I remember sitting in my third-grade class and daydreaming about fishing on the lake with Uncle Lee. I could even smell the bait and the old moldy wood boat he had. Later, I built a 52-foot fiberglass boat in my backyard.

Katelyn: What kind of boat did you work on?

John: Usually, I bought or built my own boats. I've long-lined and fished hydraulic reels in the Caribbean. We fished a strike net out of a mullet boat. I fished traps out of a crawfish boat. I've fished trawl nets on a shrimp boat. I trapped lobster when we lived in Florida on a small boat. These boats have all been various sizes and mostly built out of fiberglass or aluminum. I designed and built most of them.

Katelyn: What's one of your favorite fishing memories?

John: We had hurricanes, engine trouble, pirates, and accidents, but none of that compared to the joy I had in fishing. After the big fiberglass boat was finished, I started fishing for red snapper and grouper in the Caribbean. We'd leave Miami harbor in winter, and after two days of travel, we'd strip down to our shorts because it was always warm. The water was so crystal clear you could see hundreds of feet down.

Katelyn: What would you say to someone interested in becoming a deep sea fisher?

John: Talk to people who do it so you can learn. Get work on different boats to learn how to work the equipment and the boat. You'll need to know how to fix engines and make boat repairs. You need to learn how to navigate with nautical maps and how to read the weather. Most of all, you need to stay sharp, because fishing is one of the most dangerous jobs in the world, but I can't imagine doing anything else.

GLOSSARY

aquaculture—the farming of aquatic animals and plants

autopilot—the device that controls steering in a vehicle without constant human attention

bait—something such as food used to attract animals to a hook or into a trap

bioluminescent—the production of light by living organisms

black market—trade that is against the law

bycatch—unwanted animals that are caught

capsize—to overturn

commercial—designed mainly for profit

communication—a system for sending and receiving messages

crowbar—a strong metal lever

debris—fragments of something that has been destroyed or broken into pieces

delicacy—something pleasing to eat because it is rare or a luxury

deter—to discourage or prevent from acting

distress call—communication prompted by trouble

distributors—a business that markets and sells a product for those that produce the product

ecosystems—organisms and their environment

efficient—able to produce desired results, especially without wasting time or energy

endangered—very rare and could die out completely

harvested—gathered

hijack—to stop and steal from a moving vehicle

knot—a unit of speed used by boats; 6076 feet per hour

lured—made to be attracted to something, drawn in

nautical miles—units used to measure distance at sea; equal to 1.15 miles on land

navigation—the method of identifying position, course, and distance traveled

overfishing—decreasing the amount of a fish beyond its ability to repopulate

processing plant—a place where a product is prepared or changed from its original form to one that can be used

profession—a job or a career

quota—a share or part assigned to each member of a group

ransom—payment demanded for the freedom of a captured person

receded—moved back

run aground—hit land, either on the shore or under shallow water

straits—a narrow passage of water connecting two large bodies of water

sustainable—able to maintain life using techniques that allow for continual reuse

terrorize—to fill with fear by threat or violence

tsunami—an extremely large wave, usually produced by an underwater volcanic eruption or earthquake

vast—very great in size and extent

vessel—a ship or a boat

wheelhouse—the part of the boat where the ship's captain works

yield—to produce as a result of effort

INDEX

BIBLIOGRAPHY

Bradley, Timothy J. *Demons of the Deep.*
Teacher Created Materials, 2013.

> The pressure of the ocean can kill a human in seconds. Yet some of the most delicate creatures in the world call it their home. In this book, you will meet a vampire squid as red as blood and a crab named after the mythical yeti. Dive right in, but be careful. These creatures are hungry!

Llewellyn, Claire. *Survive at Sea (Survival Challenge).*
Silver Dolphin Books, 2006.

> If you were on a fishing vessel, could you survive at sea? Find out with the 12 challenges in this book. Try to find freshwater, deal with sharks, and cope in a storm—without ever stepping foot near the water.

Morey, Shaun. *Kids' Incredible Fishing Stories.*
Workman Publishing Company, 1996.

> Meet 35 kids just like you who came face to face with fierce and fantastic fish, reeled in bizarre catches, and broke fishing records. You'll be awed and inspired by the photographs, fun facts, and silly drawings in this book.

Woodward, John. *Voyage: Ocean.* DK Publishing, 2009.

> Take a full-speed-ahead ocean voyage. Discover mountains and trenches beneath the sea, amazing marine creatures, and the vessels fishers and explorers use above and below the surface of the sea. Each page is a glimpse through a round porthole, with colorful photos and illustrations that bring the sea to life!

MORE TO EXPLORE

Crab Fishing Facts 101
http://dsc.discovery.com/tv/deadliest-catch/

Learn all about crab fishing on this page from Discovery television's *Deadliest Catch* series. Discover the duties of every crew member aboard a crab-fishing boat, from the captain and engineer to the deckhands and greenhorn. Get the lowdown on crab-fishing facts and the top 10 superstitions at sea.

Fishing Games
http://www.kibagames.com/Fishing-games

Now you can be a fisher! Play fun fishing games from Deep Sea Fishing and Fish Hunter to Fish Mania and Trap a Tuna. These games test your accuracy and fishing skills!

Georgia Aquarium: Kids Corner
http://www.georgiaaquarium.org/explore-the-aquarium/interact/kids-corner.aspx

Stop by the Georgia Aquarium's *Kids Corner* for some ocean fun. Watch live webcams of the sharks, whales, and other sea creatures at the aquarium. Then, check out the puzzles, games, and coloring pages. You'll learn fascinating facts about sea life as you play!

National Aquaculture Association: Kids Corner
http://thenaa.net/kids-corner

Visit the National Aquaculture Association's Kids Corner to learn about fish farming. Fun illustrations make the aquaculture story come to life. Then, challenge yourself with a word search and get creative with the coloring page.

ABOUT THE AUTHOR

Katelyn Rice is a student in Las Vegas, Nevada, and a proud member of her school's ROTC program. From an early age, she had an interest in writing. She is currently in the process of writing a novel. She loves to spend weekends out on the water fishing.